FLORASCOPE

FLORASCOPE
The Secret Astrology of Flowers

TEXT BY HELEN BROWN GENTRY
PHOTOGRAPHS BY SALLY TAGG

Warwick Publishing

To Philip, an orchid for all seasons.
Fondest love, Helen

For my parents,
in appreciation for tending the garden.
With love, Sally

Florascope: The Secret Astrology of Flowers
Copyright © 2005 by Helen Brown Gentry, Sally Tagg and David Bateman Ltd.
First published in New Zealand in 2003 by David Bateman Ltd.,
30 Tarndale Grove, Albany, Auckland, New Zealand

We acknowledge the financial support of the Government of Canada through the
Book Publishing Industry Development Program for our publishing activities.

ISBN: 1-894622-67-7

Published in North America by Warwick Publishing Inc.
161 Frederick Street, Suite 200
Toronto, Ontario M5A 4P3 Canada
www.warwickgp.com

Distributed in Canada by
Canadian Book Network
c/o Georgetown Terminal Warehouses
34 Armstrong Avenue
Georgetown, Ontario L7G 4R9
www.canadianbooknetwork.com

Distributed in the United States by
CDS
193 Edwards Drive
Jackson TN 38301
www.cdsbooks.com

Design Alice Bell
Printed in China through Everbest Printing Co. Ltd.

CONTENTS

INTRODUCTION

For centuries astrologers have linked personality traits with the time of birth and the movement of the stars. They have also connected astrological signs to various crystals, animals and plant forms. The colour and form of particular blooms have often been associated with horoscope signs.

Florascope summons the stars to your own living room – right into that vase on your coffee table, bringing a playful dimension to your interconnection with nature's mystery.

Florascope enables you to see yourself and the people in your life in a different way. You probably never realised the friend who insists on taking centre stage is exhibiting her Sunflower tendencies. Or that the lawyer who lives next door is behaving like a typical Chrysanthemum when he buys an antique desk – and makes sure you never see the price tag . . .

By reading your personal Florascope, you'll unearth aspects of nature's fabulous creation that is you. You'll discover who's likely to be a compatible partner in the seed bed. You may be tempted to enhance your chances of romance by creating a dazzling arrangement mingling your Florascope flowers with those of your beloved's. Or perhaps even design your garden to encompass the Florascope signs in your family.

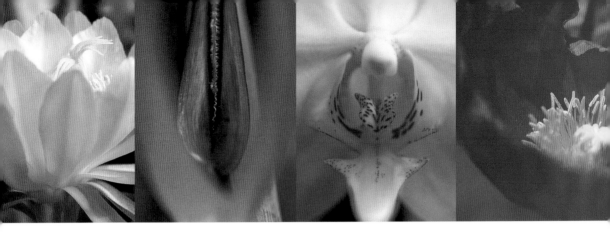

Florascope will teach you more about the children in your life, so you can better understand how to help your Lotus bud niece overcome her shyness and blossom into adulthood.

There's also the chance to meet famous blooms who sprout in your corner of the garden. Opium Poppies won't be the least surprised to find Elizabeth Taylor is one of their own species.

If for any reason you take exception to the particular flower representing you in these pages, don't drop your petals. It's probably because there are other influences in your Florascope.

A Rose who feels she is not a Rose, for instance, may well have strong Tiger Lily tendencies.

Health, career and money matters take on a different hue when viewed from a Florascope perspective. Spendthrift habits are more forgivable when you accept they're in your chlorophyll.

Once you understand your true flower spirit the garden of life will take on new magic and become a place of mystical delight.

Buddha once said that if we could see the miracle of a single flower clearly, our whole lives would change. Savour the beauty of the blooms on these pages, read a little and smile.

Tiger Lily

(Liliaceae)
21 March – 19 April
Aries

Tiger Lily

A natural leader, Tiger Lily is born to leave a mark, whether it's from sticky pollen stamens or dazzling achievements in the theatrical world. In life's bouquet, Tiger Lily aims to achieve greater heights than other flowers and is guaranteed to make an impact. Only one place suits this vivid exhibitionist – and that's first. Supercharged Tiger Lily seldom droops, except maybe at four in the morning after everyone else has folded up their petals for the night and gone home. Courageous and determined, Tiger Lily defends helpless daisies, and will fight for a cause long after softer-stemmed souls have slunk into the shadows. For all the colour and show, Tiger Lily is easily damaged by thoughtless behaviour and is the first to cry at Walt Disney movies.

Tiger Lily and money Treats the dollar as a form of energy that needs to be burned.

Health Generally too busy to be sick. Prone to broken bones and ailments of the head.

Tiger Lily in love Romantic, adoring, possessive.

Career Business executive, television director, military officer, entrepreneur, movie star, inventor, events manager, head-hunter.

Spirit Prefers religions involving theatrical expression of faith.

Tiger Lily child

Parents expecting a Tiger Lily baby had better rest up. They won't be getting much peace and quiet over the next two decades. A bud who can't wait to blossom, young Tiger Lily is an early developer who seizes life with full passion.

Although parents will be able to boast how their Tiger Lily learned to walk and crawl far sooner than the baby books predicted, they may fail to mention that they've had to put their china and other breakables in storage.

Young Tiger Lilies resent being tied to a stake and told what to do. Set them a challenge instead, and they'll reach for the stars. They must be frequently nourished with love and approval.

Flowers compatible with Tiger Lily

Magnolia | Passion Flower | Sunflower | Bird of Paradise
Orchid | Poppy | Tiger Lily

Famous
Tiger Lilies

Warren Beatty
Marlon Brando
Casanova
Charlie Chaplin
Eric Clapton
Joan Crawford
Russell Crowe
Leonardo da Vinci
Celine Dion
Aretha Franklin
Marvin Gaye
Hugh Hefner
Fred Hollows
Elton John
Lucy Lawless
Julian Lennon
Sarah Jessica Parker
Paloma Picasso
Diana Ross
Vincent van Gogh

Magnolia

(Magnoliaceae)
20 April – 20 May
Taurus

Magnolia

One species of magnolia can take ten years to bloom. The flowers, when they finally appear, are magnificent. Likewise, the Magnolia personality is willing to wait for the best. Magnolia, the careful long-term thinker, recognises quality and is usually too cautious to get ripped off by flashy salesmen.

Calm and loving, this fleshy bloom thrives in a rich compost of home comforts. A luxurious bed is an important item to someone who invented the notion of sleeping late. Magnolia loathes being uprooted and transplanted to arid neighbourhoods littered with car parts and hamburger wrappings.

This flower appreciates all the sensual aspects of life, from art galleries to aromatherapy massages, and is generally a magnificent cook. Magnolia's petals are seldom ruffled. Explosions of anger are rare – and memorable.

Magnolia and money A shrewd investor, Magnolia is willing and able to mulch cash down for a spectacular display of soft furnishings later on.
Health Magnolia is uncomplaining to the point of heroism when unwell. Vocal expression is important to this flower, and the delicate throat may be vulnerable to infection.
Magnolia in love Committed, physical, revels in pampering.
Career Botanist, stock broker, doctor, chef, architect, singer, engineer, interior designer.
Spirit Nature worship appeals.

Magnolia child

This bud is a placid baby who can seem somewhat quiet and shy. When other kids are playing dress-ups, Magnolia bud may stand in the shade and let them bask in the sunlight.

Strongly connected to nature, this baby is soothed by walks through leafy parks. Older Magnolia children usually love holidays in the wilderness.

Baby Magnolia needs lots of cuddles, but hates being smothered. An emotionally steady, loving home life provides the best growing conditions. Strict discipline tends to bring out a stubborn side. A regular supply of down-to-earth explanations and hugs will ensure Baby Magnolia becomes a prize bloom.

Flowers compatible with Magnolia

Passion Flower | Lotus | Tulip | Chrysanthemum
Poppy | Tiger Lily | Magnolia

magnolia

Famous Magnolias

Tony Blair

Cher

Penelope Cruz

Salvador Dali

Daniel Day-Lewis

Queen Elizabeth II

Ella Fitzgerald

Sigmund Freud

Pope John Paul II

Harvey Keitel

Jonah Lomu

Shirley MacLaine

Karl Marx

Willie Nelson

Jack Nicholson

Al Pacino

Eva Peron

William Shakespeare

Barbra Streisand

Passion Flower

(Passifloraceae)
21 May – 20 June
Gemini

Passion Flower

Restless Passion Flower rambles over the garden of life, dazzling others with easy charm and wit. Yearning for the exotic jungle over the back fence, this beauty may dismiss humble herbs because of a low boredom threshold.

Few species are more broad-minded and versatile. Fast-moving Passion Flower has an enviable ability to stay youthful. Insatiably curious, this bloom may poke tendrils into other people's business, making journalism a common career. Possessing amazing dexterity, Passion Flower is capable of doing two things at once.

With tendrils tucked away in foliage, neediness and vulnerability are concealed. Highly fertile, Passion Flower longs to produce fruit, yet the chances of happy-ever-after may be destroyed by serial affairs. Passion Flower secretly yearns for a soul mate.

Passion Flower and money Exquisite taste, endless debt.
Health Usually vigorous, providing there's room to move. Prone to nervous exhaustion. Hates being confined to bed.
Passion Flower in love Flirtatious, exciting, sensitive.
Career Journalist, musician, surgeon, photographer, poet, explorer, artist, politician.
Spirit Attracted to unusual sects, including speaking in tongues.

Passion Flower child

Born chatterers and natural adventurers, baby Passion Flowers have active minds and bodies. Keeping up with them can present a challenge. Passion Flower buds hate being confined to restricted areas such as playpens. They need plenty of safe space in which to explore their world.

Passion Flower buds have rich fantasy lives that occasionally get blended into reality. They should be encouraged to talk through their dreams and illusions so they learn to distinguish them from the physical world.

Flowers compatible with
Passion Flower

Magnolia | Rose | Orchid | Tiger Lily | Lotus | Passion Flower

Famous
Passion Flowers

James Brown
Joan Collins
Jacques Cousteau
Bob Dylan
Clint Eastwood
Michael J Fox
Anne Frank
Judy Garland
Paul Gauguin
Che Guevara
John F Kennedy
Nicole Kidman
Cyndi Lauper
Paul McCartney
Kylie Minogue
Marilyn Monroe
The Artist Formerly
        Known as Prince
Queen Victoria
Walt Whitman

Lotus

(Nymphaeaceae)
21 June – 22 July
Cancer

Lotus

Sensitive lotus flourishes in a calm, deep pond. A tranquil home environment is important to this complex and exquisite bloom. Prone to outlandish dreams, bursts of telepathy and psychic awakening, Lotus could float away over the horizon if not earthed with home cooking, sensible walking shoes and supermarket shopping lists.

Struggling through life's murk to the sunlight, Lotus sets high goals and attains them with the sort of determination and effort lesser flowers lack. Compassionate Lotus is easily damaged by the rush and rudeness of modern living. To cope with real and imagined cruelties, this flower may develop a tough stem and can give the appearance of spiky aggression. The essential Lotus, however, is deeply loving and caring of humanity, which is why it was Buddha's favourite flower.

Lotus and money Willing to strive for a well-paid job and a solid home.
Health May grizzle about a scratch on the knee, but endure a full bout of flu with fortitude. Watch for digestive disorders, coughs and anaemia.
Lotus in love Slow to make the first move, romantic, devoted.
Career Marine biologist, psychologist, mountaineer, diver, investor, spiritual leader, environmental engineer, aid worker.
Spirit Profound interest in spiritual matters springing from desire to ease human suffering.

Lotus child

Lotus buds often take time adjusting to kindergarten, school or any other activities designed to separate children from their mothers. Such adjustments are best made gradually with generous showers of reassurance so the child does not feel rejected.

Highly imaginative, Lotus babies blossom when encouraged to express themselves through art, music or storytelling.

Like a single Lotus in a pond, this child may seem content with its own company for long periods.

With a natural affinity for water, a fractious Lotus baby can be readily soothed in a warm bath. Older Lotus buds love swimming, sailing and water skiing.

Flowers compatible
with Lotus

Sunflower
Tulip
Cactus Flower
Poppy
Magnolia
Passion Flower
Lotus

Famous
Lotuses

Pamela Anderson

Louis Armstrong

George Bush jr

Julius Caesar

Bill Cosby

Tom Cruise

His Holiness the 14th Dalai Lama

Princess Diana

John Glenn

Jerry Hall

Tom Hanks

Ernest Hemingway

Sir Edmund Hillary

Helen Keller

Nelson Mandela

Rembrandt

Ringo Starr

Meryl Streep

Prince William

Robin Williams

Sunflower

(Asteraceae)
23 July – 22 August
Leo

Sunflower

Friendly Sunflower beams kindness and loyalty across the plant kingdom. Revelling in stardom, this dramatic bloom adores centre stage. Sunflower seems so confident, few understand how much love and attention this plant can soak up. Deprived of adoration, Sunflower withers, and may eventually even topple over. Nurtured with love, however, Sunflower exudes enough warmth and bounce to light up the neighbourhood.

It's easy to provide this beauty with the admiration required. Often taller than average, Sunflower cuts a dash with stunning hairstyles and regal fashion flair. Sex appeal is strong. A circle of friends in a stylish home filled with children completes the Sunflower scene. Throughout life this fun-lover stays in touch with the inner child, enjoying games, sport and taking risks.

Sunflower's good looks and love of laughter attract clouds of admirers, including carnivorous insects. Care must be taken not to be dazzled by bright lights.

Sunflower and money Can fritter it away on luxury items and hairdressers.
Health Generally strong. Deprived of affection, may be prone to viruses and high fever.
Sunflower in love Romantic, radiant, unrestrained.
Career Talk show host, gourmet cook, teacher, children's writer, astronaut, magazine editor, lawyer, five-star general.
Spirit Once worshipped by Incas as living sun gods, Sunflowers retain a pagan approach, finding spirituality in nature.

Sunflower child

Cheerful and sunny, baby Sunflowers are heart-warming additions to any household. Parents may be bewildered to find that their Sunflower buds hardly ever seem to run out of energy. Involvement in sports and physical activity provides a helpful outlet.

Developing a taste for parties early in life, baby Sunflowers are popular with other children, and often seem to land themselves star parts in school shows.

During the few quiet moments, parents may try to encourage baby Sunflowers to learn the gentle art of staying quiet while somebody else is talking, and maybe not to exaggerate quite so much. Dream on.

Flowers compatible with Sunflower

Tulip | Rose | Bird of Paradise | Tiger Lily
Passion Flower | Lotus | Sunflower

Famous
Sunflowers

Neil Armstrong
Lucille Ball
Napoleon Bonaparte
Fidel Castro
Julia Child
Bill Clinton
Henry Ford
Alfred Hitchcock
Dustin Hoffman
Whitney Houston
Mick Jagger
Magic Johnson
C G Jung
Jacqueline Kennedy-Onassis
Lawrence of Arabia
Madonna
Steve Martin
J K Rowling
Martha Stewart
Mae West

Tulip

(Liliaceae)

23 August – 22 September

Virgo

Tulip

Gentle and refined, Tulip cares for others at the deepest level. A compassionate heart and a bathroom cabinet full of alternative medicines are freely available to the weak and wilting. Sharp-minded Tulip stores a wealth of information on most subjects, particularly matters relating to health.

A perfectionist, Tulip keeps a tidy closet, is never late and always remembers to floss. Prone to worry, this sensitive bloom benefits from nights at the opera, theatre or concert hall, where emotions may gush freely as water from a garden hose.

Tulip is a conservative dresser, favouring subtle shades to enhance a natural dignity. Passion for hygiene and exotic bath gels ensure a lingering perfume. Inherently monogamous, Tulip often waits for the ideal partner. While seeming demure, this bulb is explosively sensuous. Once sexuality is awakened, passion is experienced in full bloom.

Tulip and money Able to save while others splurge.
Health Usually take good care of themselves. Prone to eating disorders and nervous upsets.
Tulip in love Decent, devoted, discreet.
Career Librarian, cosmetic surgeon, doctor, herbalist, dental hygienist, accountant, theatre critic, priest or nun, geneticist.
Spirit Comfortable in the local church, but may keep a pack of tarot cards at home.

Tulip child

Tulip buds hold their petals tightly
together and may seem reluctant to
burst into full bloom. Lavished with
genuine compliments and praise,
however, these shy children will
gradually unfold in pure splendour.

Eager for approval, young Tulip
crumples in the face of teasing and
criticism. Although helpful about the
house, and handy at remembering
exactly who left the keys where,
baby Tulip flourishes when introduced
to the magical worlds of fantasy
and daydreams.

Flowers compatible
with Tulip

Rose | Cactus Flower | Chrysanthemum | Magnolia
Lotus | Sunflower | Tulip

Famous
Tulips

Ingrid Bergman

Leonard Bernstein

Sir Donald Bradman

Sean Connery

Queen Elizabeth I

Greta Garbo

Richard Gere

Goethe

Hugh Grant

Michael Jackson

Gene Kelly

Stephen King

Sophia Loren

Maria Montessori

Sam Neill

Otis Redding

Peter Sellers

Mother Theresa

Fay Weldon

Rose

(Rosaceae)
23 September – 22 October
Libra

Rose

Refined and romantic Rose adores soft candlelight and lingering gazes over dinner. Nobody **glows and blushes** like Rose in love. Should concerned friends be foolish enough to point out minor shortcomings such as nose picking in the object of devotion, Rose becomes prickly and defensive.

This beauty thrives in harmonious environments free of weedy piles of dishes and heaps of dirty clothes. Rich mulches of admiration and devotion are required. In return Rose provides **perfumed sophistication** and intriguing conversation. While this bloom holds strong opinions, Rose is never afraid to suddenly take the opposing view. Should discussion develop into a compost-flinging slanging match, Rose trembles and falls apart.

This bloom has a **practical side** willing to put words into action. Unlike flowers with less integrity, Rose will actually turn up at the school cake stall or fix that dripping faucet. A lover of music and tiny animals, Rose loathes the idea of lingering single and alone in a vase. With all that charm and good looks, it's hardly likely.

Rose and money Astute with finances. Willing to lash out on luxuries.
Health These prize blooms rely on strong stalks, therefore back problems can be an issue. Kidneys and liver may require attention. Regular pampering at the beauty salon will lift skin quality, as well as mood.
Rose in love Romantic, enduring, dependent.
Career Environmentalist, diplomat, musician, computer graphics expert, interior designer, beauty therapist, art dealer, image consultant.
Spirit Believes in a loving God. Attracted to religions emphasising inner calm and global harmony.

Rose child

Among the most attractive infants, Rose buds are natural contenders for baby photo competitions. Blessed with looks and charm, they soon train adults to pander to their whims.

Faced with too many options ('Do you want a bike or a scooter for Christmas?' – 'Would you like peanut butter or honey on your sandwich?') Rose bud becomes unsettled and confused. Better to take gentle control and treat baby Rose with fairness sprung from an adult sense of logic.

Flowers compatible with Rose

Cactus Flower | Bird of Paradise | Orchid | Passion Flower
Sunflower | Tulip | Rose

Rose

Famous Roses

Brigitte Bardot
Sir Peter Blake
Catherine Deneuve
Michael Douglas
Sarah Ferguson
F Scott Fitzgerald
George Gershwin
Mahatma Ghandi
Jesse Jackson
John Lennon
Groucho Marx
Olivia Newton John
Gwyneth Paltrow
Luciano Pavarotti
Eleanor Roosevelt
Sting
Ian Thorpe
Oscar Wilde
Catherine Zeta Jones

Cactus Flower

(Cactaceae)
23 October – 21 November
Scorpio

Cactus Flower

From the harshest desert, Cactus Flower bursts forth with magnetic beauty. Likewise, the Cactus Flower personality is capable of mastering the miracle of transformation. With mystery furled in every petal, a Cactus Flower person gathers a million secrets over one lifetime, and (usually) keeps them quiet.

Those daunted by Cactus Flower's occasionally thorny exterior would do well to remember these personalities are global winners of the Self-Criticism Award. They're more likely to be fretting over their flabby chin than your shopping-bag thighs.

Willing to endure hours at the office even after the cleaners have gone home, Cactus Flower people are generally successful at achieving their goals. Enthusiastic and unshockable in matters relating to the bedroom, these blooms, when fully developed, are rumoured to be as hot as noon in Texas.

Cactus Flower and money Generally has a secret hoard tucked away.
Health Usually hardy and able to endure extremes in temperature. May experience abdominal problems.
Cactus Flower in love Passionate, intense, emotional.
Career Archaeologist, lawyer, private investigator, psychiatrist, brain surgeon, hotel manager, gynaecologist, racing driver.
Spirit Drawn to the mysterious aspects of religion.

Cactus Flower child

A loyal friend and family member, Cactus Flower buds are eager to delve into life's secret corridors. Careful parents will guide them away from forbidden Internet sites and experimental chemistry books to mainstream sources of knowledge such as science fairs and medical textbooks.

Tree huts and cubby houses are great for these children, who regain strength in quiet, solitary moments.

Steal candy from these babies at your peril. Cactus Flower buds will fight for what's theirs – and maybe raid their enemy's garden for revenge.

Flowers compatible with
Cactus Flower

Bird of Paradise | Chrysanthemum | Poppy | Lotus | Tulip
Rose | Cactus Flower

cactus

Famous
Cactus
Flowers

Marie Antoinette

Charles Atlas

Hillary Clinton

Christopher Columbus

Leonardo di Caprio

Sally Field

Jodie Foster

Bill Gates

Whoopi Goldberg

Shere Hite

Grace Kelly

Robert F Kennedy

Joni Mitchell

Claude Monet

Pablo Picasso

Julia Roberts

Theodore Roosevelt

Meg Ryan

Andy Warhol

Bird of Paradise

(Strelitziaceae)
22 November – 21 December
Sagittarius

Bird of Paradise

When life seems like a packet of weedkiller, happy-go-lucky Bird of Paradise has a delightful way of brightening even the dullest corner of the garden. Open and generous, this flower encourages others to realise how fabulous they really are.

Poised on an elegant stalk, Bird of Paradise reaches for the heavens, pondering spiritual and philosophical matters – but never long or loudly enough to become a bore. A wild flower at heart, Bird of Paradise is attracted to bungy jumping, skydiving and other terrifying sports. Happiest with an air ticket in one hand and a glass of champagne in the other, this wit loves collecting ideas, going to parties and flirting.

Oblivious to the ambitions of corporate slugs and climbers, Bird of Paradise assumes the best of others – often inadvertently improving their behaviour as a result. Bird of Paradise cheers life's bleakest moments. Perennially optimistic, this bloom regards a redundancy notice as a ticket to freedom. And is usually proved right.

Bird of Paradise and money Natural gamblers – spending comes more naturally than saving.

Health Generally hardy and energetic, but may suffer joint problems and a tendency to fall over or have accidents. Check-ups tend to be cancelled in favour of social engagements.

Bird of Paradise in love Sensual, honest, adventurous.

Career Test pilot, vet, travel writer, ski instructor, cartoonist, comedian, movie director, politician.

Spirit Contrary to their outgoing personalities, Birds of Paradise are seriously committed to spiritual growth. Capable of developing a personal form of spirituality as strong to them as any organised religion.

Bird of Paradise child

Dressed in their favourite bright colours and wearing a friendly smile, baby Birds of Paradise attract admirers from all corners of the garden. These buds love the colour and fun of fancy dress and willingly taking on the role of family clown.

Dashing Bird of Paradise babies terrify their parents by swinging from ropes, leaping from boxes and accepting alarming dares from other children. A well-stocked first aid kit may be in order.

Hardly in need of exploring their fantasy worlds any further, these babies benefit from honest explanations about life's practicalities – from handling pocket money to road safety.

Deeply attached to animals, they adore a family pet.

Flowers compatible with
Bird of Paradise

Chrysanthemum
Orchid
Sunflower
Rose
Cactus Flower
Tiger Lily
Bird of Paradise

Famous
Birds of
Paradise

Woody Allen
Jane Austen
Beethoven
Maria Callas
Winston Churchill
Noel Coward
Joe DiMaggio
Walt Disney
Bob Hawke
Jimi Hendrix
John F Kennedy jr
Bruce Lee
Harpo Marx
Bette Midler
Sinead O'Connor
Brad Pitt
Frank Sinatra
Steven Spielberg
Mark Twain

Chrysanthemum

(Asteraceae)
22 December – 19 January
Capricorn

Chrysanthemum

Noble Chrysanthemum endures long after others have drooped and faded. This intelligent realist is supported by a woody stem of practical know-how and ability to make long-term plans. Chrysanthemums are often highly successful and eventually able to indulge their taste in diamonds and leather sofas. Quality to the core, this flower abhors cheap fakes. Chrysanthemum wouldn't be seen deadheaded with a $2 Rolex. Buying gifts for such a regal friend can be challenging – if all else fails, a book, an antique inkwell or breakfast at their favourite club should suffice.

At times Chrysanthemums' views may seem somewhat critical, their standards too exacting. With the aid of a little fine wine and music, they may benefit from untying their stakes and hanging loose for a while. Chrysanthemum is a loyal friend who stands back admiringly while frillier flowers flounce their petals. A good listener with a grounded perspective, this bloom provides sensible advice for all seasons.

Chrysanthemum and money Generally an excellent financial planner. Unwilling to take risks.

Health Delicate when young – may require support from protective adults (or twiggy sticks) if exposed to harsh conditions. With adequate nurture and protection from pests, however, Chrysanthemum can outlive most other flowers.

Chrysanthemum in love Caring, faithful, sincere.

Career Engineer, television or radio producer, architect, funds manager, musician, jeweller, systems analyst, political advisor.

Spirit Comfortable with the traditions of established religion.

Chrysanthemum child

Chrysanthemum buds may seem like 45-year-olds in five-year-old bodies. Mature and sensible beyond their years, theyfind the childish games other seedlings play a trifle silly.

They loathe other buds making fun of them and would rather stay inside with a book than be outside with a gang of sports-crazy bullies. An orderly routine at home is recommended.

Flowers compatible with Chrysanthemum

Orchid | Poppy | Magnolia | Tulip
Cactus Flower | Bird of Paradise | Chrysanthemum

Famous
Chrysanthemums

Muhammad Ali
David Bowie
Cézanne
Marianne Faithfull
Mel Gibson
Stephen Hawking
Anthony Hopkins
Howard Hughes
Joan of Arc
Janis Joplin
Diane Keaton
Martin Luther King
Ricky Martin
Henri Matisse
Nostradamus
Elvis Presley
Pat Rafter
Mao Tse-tung
Tiger Woods

Orchid

(Orchidaceae)
20 January – 18 February
Aquarius

Orchid

Flourishing in a hothouse of ideas, Orchid cares deeply for humanity and is capable of inspiring others to great heights.

Unblemished by bitterness, clever Orchid triumphs over hardship. The Orchid who achieves fame glows in the spotlight while less adventurous plants stand back in awe of its **magical elegance.**

At the same time, Orchid craves an inner world of tranquillity where rainbows may be climbed and the soul nurtured. Regardless of its stunning exterior, this flower is not as confident as it seems.

An Orchid friend is thoughtful and dependable, collecting a posy of individuals who are equally radical and intellectual. Naturally scientific, this bloom takes a global view and is never bigoted or narrow-minded. But, since Orchid is **ahead of its time,** care must be taken to share those amazing ideas in full, and to remain tactful.

Orchid and money Loves the latest technology, hates being in debt.

Health Prone to sudden mysterious illnesses which disappear swiftly. Happiest in even temperatures that are neither too dry nor too damp.

Orchid in love May be commitment phobic, but faithful and loyal once the decision is made.

Career Aid worker, electronics and information technologist, television or radio presenter, scientist, writer, astrologer, ballet dancer, counsellor.

Spirit Curious about all religions, interested in combining ancient wisdoms with modern knowledge.

Orchid child

To thrive, this bud requires a calm, even-tempered household. Baby Orchid is sensitive and easily troubled by family tensions.

Although the Orchid child is always on the go and seems to have bunches of friends, parents would do well to set aside special time alone with their little flower.

Their child has extraordinary perspectives on life. Through listening, adults will build baby Orchid's confidence, which isn't as robust as it seems. Once enriched with self-esteem, Orchid bud will flourish with unique, breathtaking style. Watch out, world!

Flowers compatible
with Orchid

Poppy
Tiger Lily
Passion Flower
Rose
Bird of Paradise
Chrysanthemum
Orchid

Famous
Orchids

Alan Alda

Humphrey Bogart

Cindy Crawford

James Dean

Thomas Edison

Cathy Freeman

Abraham Lincoln

Charles Lindbergh

Bob Marley

Wolfgang Amadeus Mozart

Yoko Ono

Anna Pavlova

Leontyne Price

Franklin D Roosevelt

Amy Tan

John Travolta

Alice Walker

Oprah Winfrey

Virginia Woolf

Poppy

(Papaveraceae)
19 February – 20 March
Pisces

Poppy

Stray weeds often make a beeline for Poppy. This compassionate bloom is famed for offering sympathy and understanding, even to undeserving caterpillars. Among the most artistic of flowers, Poppy is a mystic dreamer. This sensitive soul's inspiration springs from fantasy worlds. When dreams are moulded into reality, either through creative expression or service to humanity, Poppy's true purpose is fulfilled.

Some hybrids, such as Opium Poppy, may be tempted to escape hurt and disillusionment with the aid of addictive substances. Their challenge is to delve beyond feelings of isolation and sorrow to discover the inner harmony that connects all living things.

Poppies adore indulgences, from exquisite food and wine to two-hour hydrotherapy sessions at luxurious health spas. They also enjoy shedding the trappings of conventional life to experience unusual cultures and go completely wild.

Poppy and money Non-materialistic Poppy panics at the sight of a balance sheet.
Health State of health is often linked to emotional condition. Problems with feet may occur. Non-vigorous, low-impact exercise such as yoga, walking and swimming recommended.
Poppy in love Magical, vulnerable, affectionate.
Career Actor, writer, travel agent, social worker, sailor, fortune teller, composer, food critic.
Spirit Able to strengthen connection to non-physical worlds through meditation and worship, though seldom of a conventional church-going nature.

Poppy Child

Baby Poppy is seldom seen in the centre of a posy of flower buds, and is unlikely to push forward for attention. If children are playing a fantastic game, however, it was probably young Poppy's idea that ignited their imaginations in the first place.

With tendencies to float away to magic worlds beyond the classroom, Poppy bud may be accused of daydreaming. Wise parents acknowledge this child's rich inner life, while providing quiet routines and a sense of loving security.

Flowers compatible with Poppy

Tiger Lily | Magnolia | Lotus | Cactus Flower
Chrysanthemum | Orchid | Poppy

poppy

Famous
Poppies

Douglas Adams

Chopin

Nat King Cole

Albert Einstein

Peter Fonda

Mikhail Gorbachev

George Harrison

Patti Hearst

Michaelangelo

Liza Minelli

Rupert Murdoch

Rudolph Nureyev

Renoir

Nina Simone

Sharon Stone

Elizabeth Taylor

Kiri te Kanawa

Vivaldi

Bruce Willis